Splishity Splashity Bunny

Written by Jody Silver

Illustrated by A. J. MacGregor

Happytime Books

Dutton-Elsevier Publishing Company, Inc.
New York

Copyright © MCMLXXVIII   © MCML   Text and illustrations by Dutton-Elsevier Publishing Company, Inc., New York, and Ladybird Books Ltd., Loughborough. All rights reserved. No part of this book may be reproduced or copied in any form without written permission from the publisher. Printed in the U.S.A. Happytime Books is a trademark of Dutton-Elsevier Publishing Company, Inc.   ISBN 0-525-54013-X   Library of Congress Catalog Card Number 78-66854

Benjamin poked his head out the door and looked at the wonderful-sunderful day. "How splishity-splashity the sea looks," he said. "It makes even a rabbit want to swim."

"Gulp down breakfast gobblety-gibblety. It's the best day yet for getting wet!" he said to his bunny brothers and their little sister, Bonnie.

"Let's skipperty-skamperty to Aunt Harriet's house and make our lazy cousins come along," said Benjamin. Bonnie ran as fast as she could when she heard that. Aunt Harriet's house was always full of big, juicy carrots and yummy carrot jam.

As usual, the lazy cousins were sound asleep.

"Wake up, you snoozity-sleepity bedful of bunnies! We're going for a swim."

Aunt Harriet agreed it was a superty-duperty day for getting wet. "Be careful," she said. "Don't go more than five bunny lengths out from shore." Bonnie wasn't listening.

Aunt Harriet filled a big picnic basket full of all the foods that rabbits love best – red and green apples, cottontail candy, nibble-nut bread and a big jar of carrot jam.

Benjamin grabbed the basket. "I'm the biggest bunny," he boasted. "I can carry it myself."

But halfway down the beach, Benjamin got tired. Bonnie, who wanted to stay near the food, offered to help.

"Lookity, lickity!" said the two quickest run-ahead rabbits, for they had found something in the sand. It was a green umbrella. All of the tag-along bunnies came to inspect the great find.

The umbrella was so big it took three bunnies to open it.

The day was hot, but under the umbrella it was cool as a cucumber patch.

Of course, Benjamin took charge of lunch. Bonnie's eyes grew biggedy-piggedy, and she leaned so far forward she almost fell into the basket.

When almost all the food was eaten, off came shoes and shirts, hurrity-scurrity!

Everyone wanted to be the first wet rabbit. But, as always, Benjamin was first.

Only Bonnie didn't want to get wet. She had another plan.

While the other bunnies splashed, she greedily gobbled up the rest of the lunch.

Just then a blustery-gustery wind began to blow. It toppled the green umbrella and tossed everything about.

'Hold on, Bonnie!" Benjamin shouted. 'I'll be right there!" But Bonnies was already in the air.

Up, up, up the umbrella sailed. It was now many bunny lengths high!

The other rabbits watched helplessly. Even Benjamin could not think what to do.

Suddenly, a gust of wind caught the umbrella. Gently it came to rest on the water and made a little boat for Bonnie. Splishity-splashity, the umbrella floated toward the shore.

The much-relieved little rabbits pulled her in. "Any carrot jam left?" asked Bonnie. Even Benjamin could hardly believe his ears!